First-Time Mom's Baby Memory Book

FIRST-TIME MOM'S

BABY MEMORY BOOK

RECORD PRECIOUS MOMENTS AND MEMORIES

EMILY RAMIREZ

ROCKRIDGE
PRESS

Interior and Cover Designer: Elizabeth Zuhl
Art Producer: Janice Ackerman
Editor: Samantha Barbaro
Production Editor: Emily Sheehan
Illustrations: © 2019 Made by Made

ISBN: Print 978-1-64611-663-8
R0

FOR FI AND RU

THIS MEMORY BOOK BELONGS TO

_____

AND MY BABY

_____

BORN ON

_____

The joy and anticipation of going out in public outweighed the stress of leaving the house when:

_____

_____

_____

_____

_____

The first friend you made on an outing was:

_____

_____

_____

_____

_____

My favorite place to go when I need to get out of the house is:

_____

_____

_____

_____

_____

"I'VE CONQUERED A LOT OF THINGS ... BLOOD CLOTS IN MY LUNGS—TWICE ... KNEE AND FOOT SURGERIES ... WINNING GRAND SLAMS BEING DOWN MATCH POINT ... TO NAME JUST A FEW, BUT I FOUND OUT BY FAR THE HARDEST IS FIGURING OUT A STROLLER!"

SERENA WILLIAMS

"I TELL MY DAUGHTER EVERY MORNING, 'NOW, WHAT ARE THE TWO MOST IMPORTANT PARTS OF YOU?' AND SHE SAYS, 'MY HEAD AND MY HEART.' BECAUSE THAT'S WHAT I'VE LEARNED IN THE FOXHOLE: WHAT GETS YOU THROUGH LIFE IS STRENGTH OF CHARACTER AND STRENGTH OF SPIRIT AND LOVE."

VIOLA DAVIS

One thing I'd like you to remember always is:

_____

_____

_____

_____

_____

Something you remind me of every day is:

_____

_____

_____

_____

_____

Something I tell you every day is:

_____

_____

_____

_____

_____

Calming a cranky baby isn't always as easy as picking them up. I've figured out that the secret to calming you down is:

_____

_____

_____

_____

_____

Your favorite place to sleep is:

_____

_____

_____

_____

_____

Feeling your sleeping body in my arms fills me with:

_____

_____

_____

_____

"A MOTHER'S ARMS ARE MORE COMFORTING THAN ANYONE ELSE'S."

DIANA, PRINCESS OF WALES

"SLEEP AT THIS POINT IS JUST A CONCEPT,
SOMETHING I'M LOOKING FORWARD
TO INVESTIGATING IN THE FUTURE."

AMY POEHLER

Pick one:

- O Baby sleep books are most useful as coasters for cold coffee.
- O Baby sleep books saved my sanity.

- O I didn't need baby sleep books because I successfully performed a top-secret dance on a misty lake during a harvest moon surrounded by molting bluebirds in exchange for a baby who was born a sleeper.

The first time you slept through the night was: _____ / _____ / _____ .

I did/did not sleep through the night that night:

_____

_____

_____

_____

_____

_____

Bedtime can range from unbearably tiresome to incredibly precious. Right now, bedtime in our house looks like:

_____

_____

_____

_____

One piece of advice I'd give my younger self:

_____

_____

_____

_____

_____

One piece of advice I'll pass along if you become a parent:

_____

_____

_____

_____

_____

Something I've struggled with, but have overcome by embracing the idea that, in the end, everything will be okay is:

_____

_____

_____

_____

_____

_____

"I THINK ANYTHING I WOULD TELL MY YOUNGER SELF, MY YOUNGER SELF WOULDN'T LISTEN TO ANYWAY. BUT [I WOULD PROBABLY SAY] THE SAME THING MY MOTHER TOLD ME WHEN I BECAME A NEW MOM, WHICH WAS, 'EVERYTHING'S GONNA BE OKAY. YOU'VE GOT THIS. YOU DON'T HAVE TO STRESS OR WORRY, YOU DON'T HAVE TO TAKE ANYTHING TOO SERIOUSLY.'"

JENNA FISCHER

"YOU ARE THE CLOSEST I WILL
EVER COME TO MAGIC."

SUZANNE FINNAMORE

There's nothing more magical than a baby's first giggle. The first time you giggled was:

_____

_____

_____

_____

_____

One surefire way to get you to laugh is:

_____

_____

_____

_____

_____

The most magical thing about motherhood so far has been:

_____

_____

_____

_____

_____

I did/did not name you after my seventh-grade crush:

_____

_____

_____

_____

_____

If no, here's how you got your name:

_____

_____

_____

_____

_____

One way this big, all-encompassing, molecule-deep mama love has changed relationships in my life has been:

_____

_____

_____

_____

_____

"HAVING KIDS FEELS LIKE THAT
FIRST SEVENTH-GRADE CRUSH THAT
OVERWHELMS EVERY MOLECULE IN
YOUR BODY, BUT IT'S PERMANENT."

KRISTEN BELL

"NO ONE TOLD ME I WOULD BE
COMING HOME IN DIAPERS, TOO."

CHRISSY TEIGEN

If I could wear the giant mesh hospital undies every day for the rest of my life, I'd be:

O Ecstatic

O Horrified

O I'm too tired to generate emotion about underpants

Speaking of diapers, the first time you had a diaper blowout, you were:

_____

_____

_____

_____

_____

_____

Diaper jokes aside, something else that came as a surprise in the beginning was:

_____

_____

_____

_____

_____

_____

Hands down, the most challenging part of motherhood so far has been:

_____

_____

_____

_____

_____

_____

Things started to get easier once you:

_____

_____

_____

_____

_____

_____

One thing I do for self-care when my battery is running low is:

_____

_____

_____

_____

"A STRONG WOMAN LOOKS A CHALLENGE
DEAD IN THE EYE AND GIVES IT A WINK."

GINA CAREY

"SOMETIMES WHEN YOU PICK UP YOUR CHILD
YOU CAN FEEL THE MAP OF YOUR OWN BONES
BENEATH YOUR HANDS, OR SMELL THE SCENT
OF YOUR SKIN IN THE NAPE OF HIS NECK.
THIS IS THE MOST EXTRAORDINARY THING
ABOUT MOTHERHOOD—FINDING A PIECE OF
YOURSELF SEPARATE AND APART THAT ALL
THE SAME YOU COULD NOT LIVE WITHOUT."

JODI PICOULT

You smell like:

_____

_____

_____

_____

_____

I have/have not turned into a certified baby sniffer:

_____

_____

_____

_____

_____

Right now, the family member you most closely resemble is:

_____

_____

_____

_____

_____

_____

Something I'm proud of accomplishing before becoming a mother is:

_____

_____

_____

_____

_____

My favorite mama-baby activity when it's just the two of us is:

_____

_____

_____

_____

_____

Becoming a mother changed the way I view my own parents because:

_____

_____

_____

_____

"AND (CUE MUSIC SWELL) MOTHERHOOD
TURNED OUT TO BE THE MOST MEANINGFUL
THING I'VE EVER DONE WITH MY LIFE. REALLY."

NIA VARDALOS

THE FIRST PHOTO OF US

MY CURRENT FAVORITE PHOTO OF YOU ON MY CAMERA ROLL

"A CHILD'S FIRST TEACHER IS ITS MOTHER."

PENG LIYUAN

My go-to person who tutored me on what to expect with new motherhood was:

_____

_____

_____

_____

_____

The person most likely to teach you your first curse word is:

_____

_____

_____

_____

_____

If I could teach you one thing today that you could apply tomorrow, it would be:

_____

_____

_____

_____

_____

Dressing you for the first few times was:

_____

_____

_____

_____

_____

_____

How many of these things are on my unofficial mom uniform right now:

O Tears   O Formula

O Spit-up   O Slobber

O Coffee   O Snot

O Milk   O Something I hope is chocolate

The ride home from the hospital was:

_____

_____

_____

_____

_____

"MOMS ARE LIFE'S NUMBER ONE CHEERLEADERS WITHOUT UNIFORMS."

RICHELLE E. GOODRICH

"A BABY IS SOMETHING YOU CARRY
INSIDE YOU FOR NINE MONTHS, IN YOUR
ARMS FOR THREE YEARS, AND IN YOUR
HEART UNTIL THE DAY YOU DIE."

MARY MASON

You were born before/on/after your due date:

_____

_____

_____

_____

_____

_____

The first person to meet you outside our immediate family was:

_____

_____

_____

_____

_____

_____

Something you're doing now that I don't ever want to forget is:

_____

_____

_____

_____

One thing I do now that, before I became a mom, I said I'd never do is:

_____

_____

_____

_____

_____

Something I'm currently 100 percent winging, but it works for us is:

_____

_____

_____

_____

Something I didn't understand about motherhood before becoming a mother, but now look back on and laugh at my own naïveté, is:

_____

_____

_____

_____

"IT'S FUNNY WHEN YOU THINK BACK ON THE PARENT YOU THOUGHT YOU WOULD BE BEFORE YOU HAD KIDS AND HOW YOU JUDGE OTHER PARENTS. THEN YOU GIVE IN TO THE REALITY OF IT AND JUST WING IT."

MAYA RUDOLPH

"WHETHER YOUR PREGNANCY WAS
METICULOUSLY PLANNED, MEDICALLY
COAXED, OR HAPPENED BY SURPRISE,
ONE THING IS CERTAIN—YOUR LIFE
WILL NEVER BE THE SAME."

CATHERINE JONES

The day I found out I was going to be a mama, _____ / _____ / _____ , the first person
I told was:

_____

_____

_____

_____

_____

One change your arrival forced me to make that I'm grateful for is:

_____

_____

_____

_____

_____

_____

Something from my pre-baby life I'm eager to fit back into my new life is:

_____

_____

_____

_____

The first time I really listened to and trusted my mama gut was:

_____

_____

_____

_____

_____

_____

Something you've done that has shown me how strong you are is:

_____

_____

_____

_____

_____

Strength manifests in different ways. One way I've grown stronger as a mother is:

_____

_____

_____

_____

"BIRTH IS ABOUT MAKING MOTHERS . . .
STRONG, COMPETENT, CAPABLE
MOTHERS WHO TRUST THEMSELVES AND
KNOW THEIR INNER STRENGTH."

BARBARA KATZ ROTHMAN

"HAVING AN INFANT SON ALERTS ME
TO THE FACT THAT EVERY MAN, AT ONE
POINT, HAS PEED ON HIS OWN FACE."

OLIVIA WILDE

You generally loathe/tolerate/love diaper changes:

_____

_____

_____

_____

_____

I have/have not been caught off guard and been peed on during a diaper change:

_____

_____

_____

_____

_____

_____

If I had the choice between a year's supply of diapers, a year of a laundry service, or a year of prepared dinners, I'd pick:

_____

_____

_____

_____

My absolute favorite part about your tiny little baby body is:

_____

_____

_____

_____

_____

Something about my postpartum body that makes me proud is:

_____

_____

_____

_____

_____

After childbirth, the road to full physical recovery can be a long one. My journey so far has been:

_____

_____

_____

_____

"EVEN IF IT HAS NOT BEEN YOUR HABIT
THROUGHOUT YOUR LIFE SO FAR, I
RECOMMEND THAT YOU LEARN TO THINK
POSITIVELY ABOUT YOUR BODY."

INA MAY GASKIN

"WHEN WE ENCOURAGE NEW PARENTS
TO 'TREASURE THESE MOMENTS BECAUSE
THEY DON'T LAST FOREVER,' WE NEED
TO REMEMBER TO ALSO REASSURE THEM
THAT THEY WILL SURVIVE THESE MOMENTS
BECAUSE THEY DON'T LAST FOREVER."

L. R. KNOST

If I could revisit a certain stage of your life, it would be:

_____

_____

_____

_____

_____

I have/have not been told by a random person in a grocery store to "treasure every second":

_____

_____

_____

_____

_____

The most trying baby stage so far has been:

_____

_____

_____

_____

_____

You can/cannot get around all the baby-proofing gear I installed:

_____

_____

_____

_____

_____

I can/cannot seamlessly operate all the baby-proofing gear I installed, the most absurdly difficult being:

_____

_____

_____

_____

Humor is one way to deal with the stresses of parenthood. My current coping mechanism for managing the mental load of motherhood is:

_____

_____

_____

_____

_____

"NOTHING BETTER THAN SPENDING
AN ENTIRE MORNING STARING
INTO MY BABY DAUGHTER'S EYES,
WHISPERING, 'I CAN'T DO THIS.'"

RYAN REYNOLDS

"PERFECTION ONLY EXISTS IN
BABIES AND PASTRIES."

GAYLE WRAY

The foods I craved while expecting you were:

1. _____   4. _____

2. _____   5. _____

3. _____   6. _____

The first solid food you tried was _____ on _____ / _____ / _____ .

Your favorite things to eat right now are:

_____

_____

_____

_____

A family recipe or food I'm excited to share with you as you get older is:

_____

_____

_____

_____

_____

_____

Your personality in utero most closely matched:

O Beyoncé's entire squadron of backup dancers while performing at Coachella
O Chuck Norris
O Eeyore

Now that you're here, your personality has changed/stayed the same:

_____

_____

_____

_____

_____

_____

_____

The first time you kicked, I felt:

_____

_____

_____

_____

_____

_____

_____

"EVERYTHING GROWS ROUNDER AND
WIDER AND WEIRDER, AND I SIT HERE IN
THE MIDDLE OF IT ALL AND WONDER WHO
IN THE WORLD YOU WILL TURN OUT TO BE."

CARRIE FISHER

"EVEN WHEN FRESHLY WASHED AND
RELIEVED OF ALL OBVIOUS CONFECTIONS,
CHILDREN TEND TO BE STICKY."

FRAN LEBOWITZ

You loathe/tolerate/love bath time:

_____

_____

_____

_____

_____

In general, I am/am not surprised by how messy motherhood has been,
especially when you:

_____

_____

_____

_____

_____

The biggest mess you've made so far has been:

_____

_____

_____

_____

_____

_____ / _____ / _____ was the first time I left you alone for longer than a shoddy, rushed, shampoo-less shower and it felt:

_____

_____

_____

_____

_____

You handled being away from me better/worse than I expected:

_____

_____

_____

_____

_____

Being alone feels:

_____

_____

_____

_____

_____

"MAKING THE DECISION TO HAVE A CHILD—IT'S MOMENTOUS. IT IS TO DECIDE FOREVER TO HAVE YOUR HEART GO WALKING OUTSIDE YOUR BODY."

ELIZABETH STONE

"AND THEN MY SOUL SAW YOU AND IT
KIND OF WENT 'OH, THERE YOU ARE.
I'VE BEEN LOOKING FOR YOU.'"

IAIN THOMAS

Your favorite lovey is called:

_____

_____

_____

_____

_____

Something you received as a gift from _____
that holds a lot of sentimental value is:

_____

_____

_____

_____

_____

I have/have not had the pleasure of experiencing a temporary (or permanent) loss of your
favorite lovey:

_____

_____

_____

_____

_____

YOU AND YOUR FIRST FRIEND

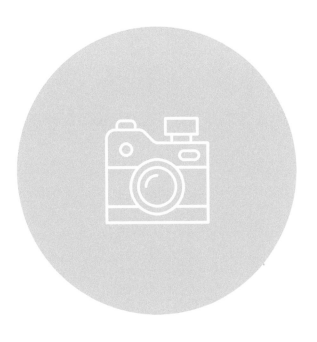

YOU AND YOUR FAVORITE LOVEY

At this point, motherhood is/is not "going by so fast":

_____

_____

_____

_____

_____

Some nicknames you have for other people in our family include:

_____

_____

_____

_____

_____

The nicknames I have for you include:

_____

_____

_____

_____

_____

"GROWN DON'T MEAN NOTHING TO A MOTHER. A CHILD IS A CHILD. THEY GET BIGGER, OLDER, BUT GROWN? WHAT'S THAT SUPPOSED TO MEAN? IN MY HEART IT DON'T MEAN A THING."

TONI MORRISON, FROM *BELOVED*

"IN ALL THE WORLD, THERE IS NO HEART
FOR ME LIKE YOURS. IN ALL THE WORLD,
THERE IS NO LOVE FOR YOU LIKE MINE."

MAYA ANGELOU

If I had to pick a song that describes how you make me feel, it would be:

_____

_____

_____

_____

_____

A place we've discovered together that now holds a special place in my heart is:

_____

_____

_____

_____

_____

Once you are older, somewhere I'm excited to explore with you is:

_____

_____

_____

_____

_____

Something I did that felt like a bit of a gamble, and that did/did not pay off, was:

_____

_____

_____

_____

_____

_____

_____

_____

_____

The first restaurant you went to was _____ on _____ / _____ / _____ .

At the restaurant, you:

- O Barfed
- O Charmed the waitstaff
- O Had a blowout
- O Refused all sources of nourishment and comfort
- O Scarred me for life
- O Scarred other people for life
- O Screamed
- O Slept
- O Tricked other people into thinking babies are a cakewalk
- O Wanted to eat the whole time
- O Were ogled by a table of elderly patrons

"[MOTHERHOOD IS] THE BIGGEST GAMBLE
IN THE WORLD. IT IS THE GLORIOUS
LIFE FORCE. IT'S HUGE AND SCARY—
IT'S AN ACT OF INFINITE OPTIMISM."

GILDA RADNER

"AH, BABIES! THEY'RE MORE THAN JUST
ADORABLE LITTLE CREATURES ON WHOM
YOU CAN BLAME YOUR FARTS."

TINA FEY

Baby farts are loud. Something else about you that is surprisingly adult-like is:

_____

_____

_____

_____

_____

The first time you smiled, you were finally reciprocating your all-encompassing, genuine love, or just tootin':

_____

_____

_____

_____

_____

I have/have not blamed you for a fart:

_____

_____

_____

_____

_____

Something I hope for your future is:

_____

_____

_____

_____

_____

The first holiday we celebrated together was:

_____

_____

_____

_____

_____

A family tradition I'm excited to share with you is:

_____

_____

_____

_____

_____

"A NEW BABY IS LIKE THE BEGINNING
OF ALL THINGS—WONDER, HOPE,
A DREAM OF POSSIBILITIES."

EDA J. LESHAN

"SEEING MY KIDS FOR THE FIRST TIME WAS PRIMAL. THE FEROCITY OF LOVE YOU FEEL FOR YOUR CHILDREN WHEN YOU SEE THEM FOR THE FIRST TIME—BUT YOU'VE KNOWN THEM INSIDE YOU—IS PHENOMENAL."

REESE WITHERSPOON

The first time I saw you, I felt:

_____

_____

_____

_____

_____

A skill you're working on mastering right now is:

_____

_____

_____

_____

_____

I'm most proud of the way you:

_____

_____

_____

_____

_____

My favorite and least favorite parts of being pregnant with or waiting for you were:

_____

_____

_____

_____

_____

You have/have not unleashed your milky fury on an unsuspecting victim. If so, who?
When it happened they:

_____

_____

_____

_____

_____

I have/have not knowingly left the house with spit-up on my shirt:

_____

_____

_____

_____

"I'VE LEARNED THAT IT'S WAY HARDER TO BE A BABY. FOR INSTANCE, I HAVEN'T THROWN UP SINCE THE '90S AND SHE'S THROWN UP TWICE SINCE WE STARTED THIS INTERVIEW."

EVA MENDES

"BECOMING A MOTHER HAS OPENED UP MY WHOLE LIFE AND GIVEN ME A WHOLE NEW PURPOSE. I FEEL LIKE A STAR AT HOME ONLY BECAUSE SHE LOVES ME SO MUCH. I MEAN, IT'S A RED CARPET EVERY DAY. IT'S WONDERFUL!"

VIOLA DAVIS

Watching you take in the world makes me feel:

_____

_____

_____

_____

_____

_____

_____

Those big beautiful baby eyes were _____ when you were born.

Your eyes are now _____ .

The first time I felt like you really looked at me was:

_____

_____

_____

_____

_____

_____

Something you've done or said that was comical but inappropriate was:

_____

_____

_____

_____

_____

Some words you hilariously mispronounce are:

_____

_____

_____

_____

_____

I am/am not to blame for exposing you to words your future teachers wouldn't appreciate:

_____

_____

_____

_____

"IT'S A BALANCING ACT. KIDS ARE REALLY SMART. THEY PICK UP ON EVERYTHING AND THEN YOU STILL HAVE TO NOT LAUGH IN FRONT OF THEM AS YOU TELL THEM THAT SOMETHING'S NOT APPROPRIATE, OR SOMETHING MIGHT BE TOO AGGRESSIVE."

MELISSA MCCARTHY

"THERE SHOULD BE A CHILDREN'S SONG: 'IF YOU'RE HAPPY AND YOU KNOW IT, KEEP IT TO YOURSELF AND LET YOUR DAD SLEEP.'"

JIM GAFFIGAN

Some of your favorite songs right now are:

_____

_____

_____

_____

_____

When I think of music from my childhood, I think of:

_____

_____

_____

_____

_____

The music I listened to most while expecting you was:

_____

_____

_____

_____

_____

One way you are showing your individuality is:

_____

_____

_____

_____

_____

When you were born, you did/did not have hair. Your hair is now:

_____

_____

_____

_____

_____

Something of myself I see in you is:

_____

_____

_____

_____

_____

"PARENTHOOD IS NOT AT ALL WHAT I
EXPECTED IT TO BE. I THOUGHT YOU MAKE
LITTLE PEOPLE IN YOUR IMAGE. BUT THEY ARE
JUST NOTHING LIKE ME OR THEIR FATHER.
THEY ARE THEIR OWN INDIVIDUALS."

REESE WITHERSPOON

"THERE'S NO WAY TO BE A PERFECT MOTHER
AND A MILLION WAYS TO BE A GOOD ONE."

JILL CHURCHILL

Something I do that you love is:

_____

_____

_____

_____

_____

Something you do that I love is:

_____

_____

_____

_____

_____

Something I'd like to improve on as a mom is:

_____

_____

_____

_____

_____

One piece of advice that worked wonders for you was:

_____

_____

_____

_____

_____

One piece of advice that worked wonders for me was:

_____

_____

_____

_____

_____

The person or place I've gone to most for advice is:

_____

_____

_____

_____

"YOU'RE GOING TO GET ADVICE FROM A LOT OF PEOPLE AND YOU CAN TAKE BITS AND PIECES, BUT YOU KNOW INNATELY WHAT YOUR CHILD NEEDS. YOU SHOULD TRUST THAT. DON'T BEAT YOURSELF UP FOR MAKING DECISIONS ABOUT THINGS THAT MAY OR MAY NOT WORK. IT'S AN EXPERIMENT IN LIFE AND YOU'RE A PART OF THAT."

LUCY LIU

"MOTHERHOOD HAS A VERY
HUMANIZING EFFECT. EVERYTHING
GETS REDUCED TO ESSENTIALS."

MERYL STREEP

I've learned the most essential thing you need to stay happy is:

_____

_____

_____

_____

The Beatles sang, "All You Need Is Love." I say, all you need is:

_____

_____

_____

_____

_____

The least essential piece of baby gear we have is:

_____

_____

_____

_____

The first non-crying sounds you made were:

_____

_____

_____

_____

_____

Each of your cries and coos really started to make sense to me when:

_____

_____

_____

_____

A song or sound I use to soothe you is:

_____

_____

_____

_____

"LOVING A BABY IS A CIRCULAR BUSINESS,
A KIND OF FEEDBACK LOOP. THE MORE YOU
GIVE THE MORE YOU GET AND THE MORE
YOU GET THE MORE YOU FEEL LIKE GIVING."

PENELOPE LEACH

YOU AT AGE _ _ _ _ _ _ _   ME AT AGE _ _ _ _ _ _ _

YOU AND SOME OF YOUR EXTENDED FAMILY

"BEING A MOM HAS MADE ME
REALLY TIRED AND SO HAPPY."

TINA FEY

The times I have felt the most and least supported in my motherhood journey have been:

_____

_____

_____

_____

_____

_____

A time when a stranger helped us was:

_____

_____

_____

_____

_____

_____

A time when we helped a stranger was:

_____

_____

_____

_____

I feel motherhood has empowered me because:

_____

_____

_____

_____

_____

_____

If humans, in general, are tender, fragile, and powerful, newborns are:

_____

_____

_____

_____

_____

_____

Becoming a mother has made me feel more like a:

O Carb-hungry, sweaty ball of emotion who   O Goddess
  just can't deal with people anymore
                                                 O Robot
O Global citizen

"MOTHERHOOD HAS TAUGHT ME HOW
EXQUISITE HUMAN BEINGS ARE AND HOW
TENDER, FRAGILE, AND POWERFUL WE ARE."

THANDIE NEWTON

"I SUCK AT SWADDLING. I DON'T KNOW
WHETHER TO USE GLASS OR PLASTIC BOTTLES.
I NEVER KNEW THERE WERE SO MANY TYPES
OF NIPPLES. AND INSTALLING A CAR SEAT
IS LIKE TAKING THE SATS! I DON'T HAVE ALL
THE ANSWERS, WHICH FEELS TERRIFYING."

GABRIELLE UNION

Something I researched intensely before you were born was:

_____

_____

_____

_____

_____

Sorry, Baby, but right now you totally suck at:

_____

_____

_____

_____

_____

_____

Sorry, Baby, but right now I totally suck at:

_____

_____

_____

_____

_____

When you wake up at 3:00 a.m., we usually:

_____

_____

_____

_____

_____

_____

If I had a magic lantern, three things I'd wish for that would be the most helpful
right now are:

1. _____

2. _____

3. _____

I have/have not Googled the answer to "Can I die from sleep deprivation":

_____

_____

_____

_____

_____

"NOBODY'S THERE WITH YOU AT 3:00
IN THE MORNING WHEN YOU'RE JUST
GOING, 'WHAT AM I DOING? WHERE DID
THEY COME FROM, AND WHEN ARE THEY
GOING?' YOU GET THROUGH IT AND
YOU FIGURE IT OUT. EVERYBODY DOES,
AND IT'S A TRIAL AND ERROR AND A WHOLE
LOT OF TEARS. AND IT'S AMAZING."

JULIA ROBERTS

"BEING A MOTHER IS LEARNING ABOUT
STRENGTHS YOU DIDN'T KNOW YOU
HAD, AND DEALING WITH FEARS
YOU DIDN'T KNOW EXISTED."

LINDA WOOTEN

The first vacation we took together was:

_____

_____

_____

_____

_____

The thing you liked most about that trip was:

_____

_____

_____

_____

_____

The thing I liked most about that trip was:

_____

_____

_____

_____

_____

In hindsight, I was/was not a good friend to those who had kids before me:

_____

_____

_____

_____

_____

You have/have not forced me to cancel plans because of an unexpected baby-related issue:

_____

_____

_____

_____

_____

I have/have not used you as an excuse to cancel plans, blaming it on a non-existent baby-related issue:

_____

_____

_____

_____

_____

"YOU DON'T TAKE A CLASS; YOU'RE THROWN INTO MOTHERHOOD AND LEARN FROM EXPERIENCE."

JENNIE FINCH

"[WHAT I LOVE ABOUT MOTHERHOOD IS] HOW MUCH FUN IT IS AND HOW I NEVER THOUGHT I COULD BE LOVED LIKE THIS OR LOVE SOMEONE SO MUCH. AND JUST THE RELATIONSHIP. THE RELATIONSHIP THAT YOU BUILD AND THAT YOU SEE GROW AS THIS PERSON BLOSSOMS IS QUITE HUMBLING AND REALLY BEAUTIFUL."

PADMA LAKSHMI

The emotions you have currently mastered include:

_____

_____

_____

_____

_____

The emotion I feel most often these days is:

_____

_____

_____

_____

_____

Looking into the future, something I'd like to do to make sure our relationship remains healthy and thriving is:

_____

_____

_____

_____

_____

On average, I shower more/less/the same as before I was a parent:

_____

_____

_____

_____

I can tell you're going through a growth spurt when:

_____

_____

_____

_____

_____

_____

The show, book, or podcast I binged on while dealing with marathon feeding sessions and long, snuggly couch naps was:

_____

_____

_____

"WHAT MOTHERHOOD SHOWS YOU
IS HOW SELFLESS YOU CAN GET. I'M
RAGGED TIRED. WHO CARES? MY
KIDS ARE HEALTHY, I'M HAPPY."

MILA KUNIS

"TRUST YOURSELF. YOU KNOW MORE
THAN YOU THINK YOU DO."

BENJAMIN SPOCK, MD

One thing I know about you that nobody else does is:

_____

_____

_____

_____

_____

Something I'm currently trying to figure out is:

_____

_____

_____

_____

_____

When I need a pep talk to boost my confidence, I:

_____

_____

_____

_____

_____

Your favorite toy right now is:

_____

_____

_____

_____

_____

A toy from my childhood I'm excited to introduce you to is:

_____

_____

_____

_____

_____

Heaven help me if someone ever gives you:

_____

_____

_____

_____

_____

"YOU WILL ALWAYS BE YOUR
CHILD'S FAVORITE TOY."

VICKI LANSKY

"SHE USED TO LOVE HER CAR SEAT AND THEN JUST ONE DAY WAS LIKE, 'I HATE IT. GOOD LUCK GETTING SOMEWHERE.' NOW I UNDERSTAND WHY SOMETIMES YOU'LL SEE MOMS AT THE AIRPORT OR IN TARGET JUST IN TEARS."

GABRIELLE UNION

Watching you grow and assert your independence is amazing, except when you randomly decided you hated:

_____

_____

_____

_____

_____

Somewhere public you've completely lost it is:

_____

_____

_____

_____

_____

Somewhere public I've completely lost it is:

_____

_____

_____

_____

_____

It's the middle of the night. You've dribbled $\frac{1}{16}$ of an ounce of urine on my PJs. My obvious next move is:

_____

_____

_____

_____

Your feelings on having $\frac{1}{16}$ of an ounce of urine in your diaper are:

_____

_____

_____

_____

I have/have not learned the hard way that we BOTH need a change of clothes in the car:

_____

_____

_____

_____

"THE BIGGEST THING I REMEMBER IS
THAT THERE WAS JUST NO TRANSITION.
YOU HIT THE GROUND DIAPERING."

PAUL REISER

"SOMETIMES I STAND THERE GOING, 'I'M NOT DOING ANY OF THIS RIGHT!' AND THEN I GET THIS BIG MAN BELCH OUT OF HER AND I GO, 'AH, WE ACCOMPLISHED THIS TOGETHER.'"

CHRISTINA APPLEGATE

When you're fussy, the order of operations for calming you is:

____ Bath	____ Go for a walk
____ Beg	____ Offer food
____ Bounce	____ Pacifier
____ Cry	____ Pass baby off to closest mammal
____ Diaper change	____ Swaddle

The secret, no-fail way to get that big old burp out of you is:

_____

_____

_____

_____

_____

_____

_____

_____

_____

_____

On average, I think, "I'm not doing any of this right!" _____ times per _____ .

My most notable mom-brain moment was:

_____

_____

_____

_____

_____

_____

_____

Your current age is: _____ .

I have/have not forgotten your exact birthdate under pressure:

_____

_____

_____

_____

_____

_____

_____

"ONE THING THEY NEVER TELL YOU ABOUT CHILD RAISING IS THAT FOR THE REST OF YOUR LIFE, AT THE DROP OF A HAT, YOU ARE EXPECTED TO KNOW YOUR CHILD'S NAME AND HOW OLD HE OR SHE IS."

ERMA BOMBECK

"CHILDREN ARE NOT ONLY INNOCENT AND
CURIOUS BUT ALSO OPTIMISTIC AND JOYFUL
AND ESSENTIALLY HAPPY. THEY ARE, IN SHORT,
EVERYTHING ADULTS WISH THEY COULD BE.

CAROLYN HAYWOOD

Getting a second chance to experience childhood at this stage in my life feels:

_____

_____

_____

_____

_____

Innocence, curiosity, optimism, joy, and happiness are all well and good, but the other side of that coin for you is:

_____

_____

_____

_____

_____

If I could be a baby for one day, the thing I'd be most excited about is:

_____

_____

_____

_____

_____

OUT ON ONE OF OUR ADVENTURES

OUR FIRST VACATION

"ENJOY THE LITTLE THINGS, FOR ONE
DAY YOU MAY LOOK BACK AND REALIZE
THEY WERE THE BIG THINGS."

ROBERT BRAULT

Something little but magical you're doing right now is:

_____

_____

_____

_____

_____

The first time I noticed you doing something entirely and uniquely you was:

_____

_____

_____

_____

_____

My favorite little thing that makes you *you* is:

_____

_____

_____

_____

_____

_____

The way you currently communicate "no" to me is:

_____

_____

_____

_____

_____

_____

In all honesty, motherhood has been more _____ and less _____
than I thought it would be.

A motherhood fantasy I've had to shelve (at least for now) is:

_____

_____

_____

_____

_____

_____

_____

"BEING A MOTHER IS AMAZING, OF COURSE.
BUT IT IS ALSO BRUTAL AND PAINFUL. MAKE
SOME SPACE FOR THE WHOLE SPECTRUM
OF FEELINGS THAT ARE ABOUT TO PUSH
IN. NOT JUST THE FANTASY ONES."

MAGGIE GYLLENHAAL

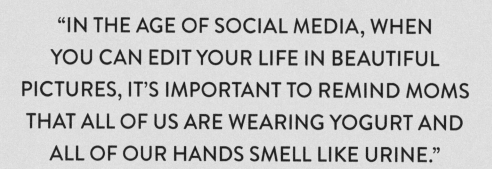

"IN THE AGE OF SOCIAL MEDIA, WHEN
YOU CAN EDIT YOUR LIFE IN BEAUTIFUL
PICTURES, IT'S IMPORTANT TO REMIND MOMS
THAT ALL OF US ARE WEARING YOGURT AND
ALL OF OUR HANDS SMELL LIKE URINE."

KRISTEN BELL

You are/are not included in my current social media presence:

_____

_____

_____

_____

_____

_____

As it stands, you're going to have to be _____ years old before you get to have your own social media accounts.

I do/do not currently have yogurt on my clothes:

_____

_____

_____

_____

_____

_____

Of course I feel terrible about it, but there was this time I accidentally:

_____

_____

_____

_____

_____

_____

_____

_____

_____

Your head has made accidental contact with:

○ A door jamb   ○ The crib rail
○ An elbow   ○ The floor
○ My head   ○ _____
○ The car frame   ○ _____

I have dropped the following foods on your head:

○ Dip   ○ Salsa
○ Eleventyhundred crumbs   ○ _____
○ Ice cream   ○ _____
○ Ketchup   ○ _____

"YOU'D BE SURPRISED HOW DURABLE
BABIES ARE. YOU HOLD THEM LIKE THEY'RE
FABERGÉ EGGS, AND THEN—WONK!—SHE
HITS HER HEAD ON THE TABLE AND YOU
THINK, 'OH MY GOSH, DID I GIVE HER A
DENT ON HER HEAD THAT'S GOING TO BE
THERE FOREVER?' BUT BABIES AREN'T THAT
PRECIOUS. EVERYONE TURNS OUT FINE."

JIMMY FALLON

"IF IT'S NOT SUPPORTIVE, POSITIVITY,
OR COFFEE . . . I DON'T WANT IT."

JANUARY HARSHE

If I could have one thing dropped on my doorstep this second, it would be:

_____

_____

_____

_____

_____

A positive mantra I would share with you is:

_____

_____

_____

_____

_____

If I could have a big ol' cup of something right now, it'd be:

_____

_____

_____

_____

_____

Your favorite books right now are:

_____

_____

_____

_____

_____

My favorite books to read to you right now are:

_____

_____

_____

_____

_____

Of all the ways motherhood has changed me, the most dramatic shift has been:

_____

_____

_____

_____

_____

"EVERYTHING I SEE, I NOW SEE THROUGH A MOTHER'S EYES. I ALWAYS SAY, YOU NEVER KNOW HOW MUCH YOUR PARENTS LOVED YOU UNTIL YOU HAVE A CHILD TO LOVE."

JENNIFER HUDSON

"IN THE EXTERNAL SCHEME OF THINGS,
SHINING MOMENTS ARE AS BRIEF AS
THE TWINKLING OF AN EYE, YET SUCH
TWINKLINGS ARE WHAT ETERNITY IS MADE
OF—MOMENTS WHEN WE HUMAN BEINGS
CAN SAY, 'I LOVE YOU,' 'I'M PROUD OF
YOU,' 'I FORGIVE YOU,' 'I'M GRATEFUL FOR
YOU.' THAT'S WHAT ETERNITY IS MADE OF:
INVISIBLE IMPERISHABLE GOOD STUFF."

MR. ROGERS

The way you say, "I love you" right now looks like:

_____

_____

_____

_____

_____

Thinking about all the "invisible imperishable good stuff" you already do makes my heart:

_____

_____

_____

_____

_____

Motherhood has made me grateful for:

_____

_____

_____

_____

_____

The way you currently get from point A to point B is:

_____

_____

_____

_____

_____

_____

My preferred way to get you from point A to point B is:

O Stroller   O Wrap

O Arms   O Dog sled

Someone from my past who I think about more often since becoming a mother is:

_____

_____

_____

_____

_____

"BIOLOGY IS THE LEAST OF WHAT MAKES SOMEONE A MOTHER."

OPRAH

"THE LIFE OF A MOTHER IS THE LIFE
OF A CHILD: YOU ARE TWO BLOSSOMS
ON A SINGLE BRANCH."

KAREN MAEZEN MILLER

You teach me selflessness and humility by:

_____

_____

_____

_____

_____

I plan to teach you selflessness and humility by:

_____

_____

_____

_____

_____

Something I love doing for you that I didn't expect is:

_____

_____

_____

_____

_____

DECKED OUT FOR OUR FIRST HOLIDAY CELEBRATION

YOU EATING—OR, MORE ACCURATELY, WEARING—SOMETHING DELICIOUS

Your little fingers and toes are special, and loved, and perfect, but cutting your nails is:

_____

_____

_____

_____

_____

_____

My perfect day with you would look like:

_____

_____

_____

_____

_____

_____

The thing that makes me feel more like myself is:

O Hot meal   O _____

O Hot night on the town   O _____

O Hot shower   O _____

O Hot stone massage

"NO MATTER WHAT YOU LOOK LIKE OR THINK
YOU LOOK LIKE, YOU'RE SPECIAL AND LOVED
AND PERFECT JUST THE WAY YOU ARE."

ARIEL WINTER

"I SEE CHILDREN AS KITES. YOU SPEND A LIFETIME TRYING TO GET THEM OFF THE GROUND. YOU RUN WITH THEM UNTIL YOU'RE BOTH BREATHLESS. THEY CRASH . . . YOU ADD A LONGER TAIL . . . YOU PATCH AND COMFORT, ADJUST AND TEACH. YOU WATCH THEM LIFTED BY THE WIND AND ASSURE THEM THAT SOMEDAY THEY'LL FLY."

ERMA BOMBECK

Speaking of flying, you have/have not flown on an airplane yet:

_____

_____

_____

_____

_____

_____

If I could fly somewhere today, I'd go to _____ with _____
and do some serious:

_____

_____

_____

My parenting style could best be described as:

_____

_____

_____

_____

_____

_____

You currently wear a size _____ , have _____ teeth, and say _____ words.

A behavior I'm making a conscious effort to model for you is:

_____

_____

_____

_____

_____

_____

_____

Besides my tolerance for infrequent showering, something else that's grown since becoming a mother is:

_____

_____

_____

_____

_____

_____

_____

"IT'S NOT ONLY CHILDREN WHO GROW.
PARENTS DO, TOO. AS MUCH AS WE WATCH
TO SEE WHAT OUR CHILDREN DO WITH
THEIR LIVES, THEY ARE WATCHING US TO
SEE WHAT WE DO WITH OURS. I CAN'T TELL
MY CHILDREN TO REACH FOR THE SUN.
ALL I CAN DO IS REACH FOR IT, MYSELF."

JOYCE MAYNARD

"OFTEN WHEN YOU THINK YOU'RE AT
THE END OF SOMETHING, YOU'RE AT THE
BEGINNING OF SOMETHING ELSE."

MR. ROGERS

A transition we are currently working through is:

_____

_____

_____

_____

_____

The mythical creature you turn into when you're teething or fighting an illness most closely resembles:

_____

_____

_____

_____

_____

Before having children, the idea of a snot vacuum sounded hideously unnecessary. My current feelings toward snot vacuums are:

_____

_____

_____

_____

I love you SO MUCH that I tolerate it when you:

_____

_____

_____

_____

_____

The thing that powers me through long nights and early mornings is:

_____

_____

_____

_____

_____

Five words that describe my love for you are:

1. _____

2. _____

3. _____

4. _____

5. _____

"I HAVE LEARNED NOT TO WORRY
ABOUT LOVE; BUT TO HONOR ITS
COMING WITH ALL MY HEART."

ALICE WALKER

"WHEN A KID WALKS IN A ROOM, YOUR CHILD OR ANYBODY ELSE'S CHILD, DOES YOUR FACE LIGHT UP? THAT'S WHAT THEY'RE LOOKING FOR."

TONI MORRISON

Both my face and my heart light up anytime you:

_____

_____

_____

_____

_____

Someone who loves you like their own child, but isn't family is:

_____

_____

_____

_____

_____

Someone I love like my own child who isn't family is:

_____

_____

_____

_____

You are already asserting your independence by:

_____

_____

_____

_____

_____

I define parental success as:

_____

_____

_____

_____

_____

I totally do/do not envision myself being the mother from *Love You Forever,* who uses a ladder to sneak into her son's room and rock him to sleep, even as a full-grown adult:

_____

_____

_____

_____

"PARENTS RARELY LET GO OF THEIR CHILDREN, SO CHILDREN LET GO OF THEM. THEY MOVE ON. THEY MOVE AWAY. THE MOMENTS THAT USED TO DEFINE THEM—A MOTHER'S APPROVAL, A FATHER'S NOD—ARE COVERED BY MOMENTS OF THEIR OWN ACCOMPLISHMENTS. IT IS NOT UNTIL MUCH LATER, AS THE SKIN SAGS AND THE HEART WEAKENS, THAT CHILDREN UNDERSTAND; THEIR STORIES, AND ALL THEIR ACCOMPLISHMENTS, SIT ATOP THE STORIES OF THEIR MOTHERS AND FATHERS, STONES UPON STONES, BENEATH THE WATERS OF THEIR LIVES."

MITCH ALBOM

"WHILE WE TRY TO TEACH OUR CHILDREN
ALL ABOUT LIFE, OUR CHILDREN TEACH
US WHAT LIFE IS ALL ABOUT."

ANGELA SCHWINDT

Since becoming a mother, the most important things you've taught me are:

_____

_____

_____

_____

_____

I hope you never get too caught up in:

_____

_____

_____

_____

_____

The most important thing I can teach you is:

_____

_____

_____

_____

_____

You have the most fun when we're:

_____

_____

_____

_____

_____

The part of being your mother that's been the most fun so far has been:

_____

_____

_____

_____

_____

Somewhere fun I want to take you when you're older is:

_____

_____

_____

_____

_____

"ONE THING I HAD LEARNED FROM WATCHING
CHIMPANZEES WITH THEIR INFANTS IS
THAT HAVING A CHILD SHOULD BE FUN."

JANE GOODALL

"IF I HAD MY CHILD TO RAISE ALL OVER AGAIN, I'D FINGER PAINT MORE, AND POINT THE FINGER LESS. I'D DO LESS CORRECTING AND MORE CONNECTING. I'D TAKE MY EYES OFF MY WATCH, AND WATCH WITH MY EYES. I WOULD CARE TO KNOW LESS, AND KNOW TO CARE MORE. I'D TAKE MORE HIKES AND FLY MORE KITES. I'D STOP PLAYING SERIOUS, AND SERIOUSLY PLAY. I WOULD RUN THROUGH MORE FIELDS, AND GAZE AT MORE STARS. I'D DO MORE HUGGING AND LESS TUGGING. I WOULD BE FIRM LESS OFTEN, AND AFFIRM MUCH MORE. I'D BUILD SELF-ESTEEM FIRST, AND THE HOUSE LATER."

DIANA LOOMANS

Pick one:

- ○ You're a good baby doing the best you can.
- ○ You're a good baby doing the best you can.
- ○ You're a good baby doing the best you can.

Pick one:

- ○ I'm a good mom doing the best I can.
- ○ I'm a good mom doing the best I can.
- ○ I'm a good mom doing the best I can.

In hindsight, the things I'd worry less about and those I'd focus more on are:

_____

_____

_____

_____

_____

_____

_____

_____

_____

About the Author

EMILY RAMIREZ is a part-time writer and a full-time mom living in the Pacific northwest. She started a humorous parenting blog a year after her first child was born because she was tired of crying in her glider while her toddler covered the bathroom in toothpaste. Her work can be found on many parenting websites, as well as her very neglected blog, *Hold Me, Don't Hold Me* (holdmedontholdmeblog.com).

CPSIA information can be obtained
at www.ICGtesting.com
Printed in the USA
LVHW072048180320
650483LV00002B/4

9 781646 116638